CW00815762

The Wheat Free Solution (Vol. 1)

Low Cost, Easy Recipes to Lose Weight and Regain
Your Vitality

Other Books by Morgan White

Disclaimer

Effort has been made to ensure that the information in this book is accurate and complete. However, the author and the publisher do not warrant the accuracy of the information, text and graphics contained within the book due to the rapidly changing nature of science, research, known and unknown facts. The author and the publisher do not hold any responsibility for errors, omissions or contrary interpretation of the subject matter herein. This book is presented solely for motivational and informational purposes only.

Table of Contents

Before You Start

Hello!

If this is the first time you read any volume of _The Wheat Free Solution_ collection just keep reading!

However if you already read volume 2, feel free to skip the following chapters: Introduction, Wheat Substitutes, Conversions. Just go right to the recipes section!

Enjoy!

Introduction

The purpose of this eBook is to offer you a great variety of low-cost, easy and tasty wheat-free recipes!

You'll also find in this chapter the reasons why you should adopt a more wheat-free lifestyle.

So, why is wheat being bashed nowadays? It has fed us for so many centuries. What seems to be the problem now?

Well, today's wheat is different from what it was 50 years ago. In order to make it hardier, shorter and better growing scientists began cross-breeding it. The idea behind this process had good intentions. However this process added some compounds to wheat that aren't healthy for human beings such as sodium azide (a known toxin) and wheat germ agglutinin (WGA). Even in small quantities, WGA may be immunotoxic, cardiotoxic, pro-inflammatory, and even neurotoxic.

Needless to say that those with celiac disease need to stay away from wheat and everything that contains gluten, because their small intestine is unable to properly digest it.

You might be asking: "But I don't have celiac disease. What does that has to do with me?"

Glad you asked!

The problem is that wheat is being increasingly blamed for the onset of other health conditions, like obesity, heart disease and a host of digestive problems including the dramatic rise in celiac-like disorders.

Cardiologist Dr. William Davis, and bestseller author of the "Wheat Belly: Lose the Wheat, Lose the Weight, and Find Your Path Back To Health" explains that the glycemic index of wheat is extremely high because it contains amylopectin A, which is more efficiently converted to blood sugar than just about any other carbohydrate, including table sugar.

Two slices of whole wheat bread increases blood sugar levels higher than a single candy bar!

This is a sure way to get that nasty deep visceral fat growing!

Phytates are also a problem, a compound that's found within the hulls of nuts, seeds, and grains. Phytic acid cannot be digested by humans. And worse, it binds to metal ions like calcium, magnesium, zinc, and iron. In turn, these minerals cannot be properly absorbed after eating – which can lead to anemia and osteoporosis.

On the subject of the adverse effects of wheat consumption, Dr. William Davis has found a wealth of clinical studies that document heart diseases, neurologic impairments, and also other problems such as diabetes, arthritis and cataracts (these last 3 related to the process of glycation via amylopectin A).

According to him there are no nutrient deficiencies as a result of the elimination of wheat, provided that you replace it with healthy foods like nuts, meats, vegetables, eggs, olives, cheese, avocados and healthy oils.

Quoting Dr. William Davis: "It is not my contention that it is in everyone's best interest to cut back on wheat; it is my belief that complete elimination is in everyone's best health interests" and "In my view, that's how bad this thing called 'wheat' has become."

Dr. Marcia Alvarez, who specializes in nutritional programs for obese patients, is quoted by nutritionist Natasha Longo:

"Modern wheat grains could certainly be considered as the root of all evil in the world of nutrition since they cause so many documented health problems across so many populations in the world."

"In my practice of over two decades, we have documented that for every ten people with digestive problems, obesity, irritable bowel syndrome, diabetes, arthritis and even heart disease; eight out of ten have a problem with wheat. Once we remove wheat from their diets, most of their symptoms disappear within three to six months".

Even though this is bad it can actually mean good news   for   you!   Why? Because it means that if you remove wheat from your diet for just some weeks you will be able to experience better well being and quality of life!

So, what are you waiting for?

Let's get this party started!

Wheat Substitutes

All the recipes contained in this eBook are, of course, wheat-free.

But I don't want you to stop here. I want you to get familiar with the most alternatives possible so that you can use your imagination and create your own tasty recipes!

When it comes to <u>cereal grains</u> you have some options such as corn, oats, rye, barley, millet, sorghum, rice, wild rice and teff.

Note: people with a gluten allergy must also avoid oats, rye and barley.

As for <u>non-cereal grains</u> you have quinoa, amaranth and buckwheat (even though the name "buckwheat" sounds wheat-related it's not). Quinoa, amaranth and buckwheat are gluten-free which means that they are not suited for the making of leavened bread, but they make awesome cookies and quick breads.

When it comes to <u>flour substitutes</u> you have a lot of options:

Brown rice flour, White rice flour, Potato starch flour, Amaranth flour, Tapioca flour, Chia flour, Buckwheat flour, Sorghum Flour, Rice flour, Chick pea flour (also known as gram or garbanzo flour), Arrowroot flour, Teff flour, Maize flour, Sorghum flour, Millet flour, Corn flour, Quinoa flour, Soya flour, Hemp flour.

Note: Barley flour, Oat Flour, and Rye Flour are not gluten-free, <u>just wheat-free</u>.

When it comes to Bean flours, even though they are a wheat-free option, they are very hard to digest and, for a lot of people, indigestible.

If you're looking for flour substitutes for cookies and cakes, ground nuts such as hazelnuts, walnuts and almonds are awesome. Just make sure that you grind them in a food processor just prior to use because they have a brief shelf life.

You want to thicken sauces and gravy?

No problem!

Use Cornstarch, Potato Starch, Tapioca, Arrowroot powder or Rice flour.

Is beer an ingredient in your recipe? Use apple juice or wine instead.

With this information and some imagination there is no stopping to your recipe creation!

Have fun in the process!

Conversions

1 cup = 237 ml (milliliters)

1 teaspoon = 5 ml

1 tablespoon = 15 ml = 3 teaspoons

1 Oz (liquids) = 30 ml

8 Oz (liquids) = 1 cup

1 Oz = 28 grams

1 inch = 2.54 cm (centimeters)

1lb. = 454 gr. (grams)

1 quart = 946 ml

4 cups = 1 quart

1 pint = 550 ml

WHEAT FREE BREAKFAST RECIPES

Walnut, apple and bacon hash

Serving: 2

Ingredients:

- 1 large apple, by your choice, sliced
- 1 cup diced pumpkin, caned
- 3 bacon strips
- ¼ cup scallion, chopped
- ¼ teaspoon nutmeg, ground
- Freshly ground salt and pepper, to taste
- Handful of walnuts, chopped

Preparation method:

1. Heat a large skillet over medium high and add chopped bacon.
2. Cook until crispy and drain excess fat.
3. Set aside to cool and break in pieces.
4. Add sliced apple, nutmeg and drained pumpkin in the same skillet in which bacon was cooked.
5. Cook until apples are soften and start to release liquid. Add scallions, and cook for 3 minutes more.
6. Finally add bacon bites and season with salt and pepper. Toss couple times to combine and serve while still hot.

Wheat-free pancakes

Serving: 2

Ingredients:

- 2 eggs
- ¼ cup milk
- 2 tablespoons almond flour
- 3 tablespoons coconut flour
- ½ teaspoon baking soda
- Small pinch of salt
- 1 ripe banana, sliced
- ¼ cup raisins
- Canola oil – for frying

Preparation method:

1. Combine all "wet" ingredients in a bowl; eggs and milk and add salt. Whisk all until eggs is fluffy and foamy.
2. Gradually stir in "dry" ingredients, coconut flour, almond flour and baking soda. Set aside in refrigerator for half an hour.
3. Heat oil in large non-stick skillet over medium high heat. Scoop the batter and pour in the skillet. Sprinkle with raisins and add couple banana slices. Cook for 1 minute or until the pancake is fluffed up.

4. Carefully flip the pancake and cook for 30 seconds on the other side.
5. Repeat the process until there is no batter left.
6. Serve immediately and eat while still hot.

NOTE: You can additionally drizzle pancakes with honey.

Wheat-free granola

Serving: 2

Ingredients:

- ½ cup oats
- 2 tablespoons sunflower seeds
- 2 tablespoons pecan nuts, chopped
- 1 tablespoon coconut flakes, unsweetened
- 2 tablespoons honey
- 1 tablespoon butter
- 2 tablespoons maple syrup
- ¼ cup pumpkin seeds
- 2 tablespoons sunflower oil
- ½ cup raisins

Preparation method:

1. Preheat the oven to 120C/240F and line baking tray with parchment paper.
2. In a large bowl combine oats, pumpkin seeds, pecan nuts, coconut flakes and sunflower seeds.
3. In a small sauce pan combine the oil, butter, maple syrup and honey. Melt over medium-high heat and stir until well combined.
4. Pour over prepared seeds and toss couple times until well coated.Spread over parchment paper.

5. Place in the oven for 2 hours. After 30 minutes gently stir the granola and place back in the oven.
6. Once the granola is baked add raisins and some other fruit if like.
7. Place in airtight container and to make simple breakfast just combine with yogurt and fresh fruits.

Wheat-breakfast energy slice

Serving: 6

Ingredients:

- 2 cups brown rice puffs
- 2 cups chopped dates
- 2 eggs
- ¼ cup brown sugar
- 1/3 cup rice flour
- ¼ cup vegetable oil

Preparation method:

1. Preheat the oven to 160C/320F and line baking tray with parchment paper.
2. Combine rice puffs, dates, sugar and rice flour in a bowl.
3. Whisk the eggs and oil in a small bowl.
4. Combine eggs with dry ingredients and stir with a wooden spoon until well combined.
5. Spoon the mixture onto baking sheet and use the back of the metal spoon to press slightly.
6. Bake in preheated oven for 30 minutes until puffed and golden.
7. Cool before slicing.

NOTE: Energy bars can be quite expensive and if you decide to make your own homemade version, you will save up some money, so we can say this is a budget friendly meal.

Banana muffins
Wheat-free

Serving: 12

Ingredients:

- 2 ripe bananas
- ¼ cup sugar
- ¼ cup yogurt
- 2 eggs
- 1 tablespoon butter
- 1 cup rice flour
- 2 teaspoons baking powder
- 1 teaspoon vanilla extract

Preparation method:

1. Preheat the oven to 180C/350F and line 12-hole muffin tin with paper cases.
2. Peel bananas and mash with a fork.
3. Mix bananas with yogurt, eggs, sugar and butter in a bowl.
4. Add baking powder and flour. Stir well until combined.
5. Spoon the mixture into paper cases to 2/3 full and bake in the oven for 20 minutes.
6. Leave on wire rack to cool before serving.

Wheat-free bagels

Serving: 8

Ingredients:

- ½ cup rice flour
- ½ cup tapioca flour
- 3 egg whites
- 2 tablespoon butter, melted
- Small pinch of salt
- 1 tablespoon honey + 2 tablespoon for coating
- ½ orange zest
- 1 tablespoon dried yeast
- ½ cup water

Preparation method:

1. Place rice flour, tapioca flour, egg whites, yeast and water in food processor.
2. Add 1 tablespoon honey and melted butter. Pulse until well combined.
3. Remove the batter and knead on floured surface for 5 minutes. If needed add more rice flour.
4. Divide dough in 8 portions and form balls from the dough, pressing them slightly and poke a hole in the center and widen it.

5. Arrange bagels on parchment paper and cover with plastic foil. Let them sit in warm room for 40-50 minutes or until they double up.
6. Bring 2 cups of water to boil and add 2 tablespoons honey and orange zest.
7. When water starts to boil add raised bagels in, and cook for 30 seconds. Then carefully flip on the other side and cook for 30 seconds more.
8. Remove bagel and place on kitchen towel.
9. When all bagels have been boiled, place them on parchment paper and bake in preheated oven at 180C/350F for 20 minutes.
10. Serve when cooled slightly.

Wheat-free blueberry pancakes

Serving: 2

Ingredients:

- 2 eggs
- ¼ cup milk
- 1 tablespoon honey
- ¼ cup coconut flour
- ¼ cup frozen berries, thawed
- Canola oil – for frying

Preparation method:

1. In a large bowl whisk eggs until fluffy.
2. Add milk and honey. Stir well to combine.
3. Fold in coconut flour and stir well until almost combined.
4. Add blueberries and gently stir in.
5. Heat a small amount of canola oil in non-stick pan.
6. Spoon the batter into heated pan; 1 tablespoon per one pancake.
7. When bubbles appear flip pancakes to other side and cook until golden.
8. Serve immediately.

Rice pudding with cinnamon

Serving: 2

Ingredients:

- 1 cup cooked cold rice
- 3 cup milk
- ¼ cup caster sugar
- 1 teaspoon cinnamon
- 1 vanilla bean, scarped seed
- Small pinch of salt

Preparation method:

1. Combine milk, sugar and cinnamon in small sauce pan.
2. Heat over medium high heat and when starts to simmer add cooked rice.
3. Cook for 5 minutes and add vanilla seeds.
4. Simmer for 2 minutes and remove from heat.
5. Serve while still hot in a small bowls.

Yogurt with berries and nuts

Serving: 2

Ingredients:

- 1 cup yogurt
- ¼ cup frozen blueberries, thawed
- ¼ cup chopped nuts
- 1 tablespoon oatmeal

Preparation method:

1. Combine all ingredients in a bowl.
2. Let them sit for 1 hour, so oat meal can be soft.
3. Serve and enjoy.

Hard boiled eggs with asparagus

Serving: 4

Ingredients:

- 4 eggs
- 1 tablespoon olive oil
- Freshly ground salt and pepper
- 1 small bunch asparagus, trimmed

Preparation method:

1. Place eggs in pot with cold water.
2. Bring to boil, and let it boils for 3 minutes.
3. Remove from the heat and let the eggs sit for 8-10 minutes. Rinse under cold water and peel the eggs.
4. Slice eggs and place in a bowl.
5. Meanwhile, prepare asparagus; place trimmed asparagus in the pot with boiling water.
6. Simmer asparagus for 5 minutes and drain. Cut into 1-inch pieces and combine with the eggs.
7. Season with salt and pepper and olive oil.
8. Toss to combine and serve.

Peanut butter and oatmeal slices

Serving: 6

Ingredients:

- 1 cup cooking oat
- 2 tablespoons sugar
- ½ teaspoon baking powder
- Small pinch of salt
- 1 teaspoon vanilla extract
- ¼ cup milk
- 1 egg, beaten
- 1 small banana, mashed
- ¼ cup peanut butter

Preparation method:

1. Preheat the oven to 180C/350F and line baking tray with parchment paper.
2. Combine cooking oat, sugar salt and baking powder.
3. Add peanut butter and banana. Stir well until combined.
4. Spread the mixture onto prepared baking sheet and flatten with spatula.
5. Bake for 20-22 minutes or until golden.
6. Cut into squares and keep in airtight container.

Muffin-like eggs

Serving: 6

Ingredients:

- 6 eggs
- 8 oz. grated cheese – by your choice
- Olive oil
- Freshly ground salt and pepper
- 6 slices non-wheat bread
- 2 garlic cloves
-

Preparation method:

1. Preheat the oven to 180C/350F and line 6-hole muffin tin with olive oil.
2. Crack the eggs into muffin holes and season with salt and pepper.
3. Top the eggs with grated cheese and bake for 15 minutes or until the eggs are set
4. Meanwhile, cut bread slices, so you have 12 pieces and toast them. When eggs are cooled remove them from muffin tin.
5. Rub garlic cloves onto toasted bread slices. Place 1 egg per 1 slice and sandwich with another slice.
6. You can additionally toast them as well.
7. Serve and enjoy.

Crusted bacon

Serving: 9

Ingredients:

-   18 bacon slices
-   ½ cup cornmeal
-   4 tablespoons brown sugar
-   Freshly ground pepper
-   2 eggs, whisked
-   ½ teaspoon ground ginger

Preparation method:

1. Preheat the oven to 200C/400F and line baking tray with parchment paper.
2. Whisk eggs in a large bowl.
3. Combine cornmeal, ground ginger, brown sugar and pepper in shallow dish.
4. Dip the bacon slices into the eggs and into prepared cornmeal mixture, removing the excess.
5. Arrange bacon slices onto baking sheet or even wire rack.
6. Bake for 40 minutes until browned and crisp.
7. Let it cool for 5 minutes before serving.

Simple breakfast smoothie

Serving: 2

Ingredients:

- 2 apricots, seeded
- 2 bananas, peeled
- 1 cup frozen blueberries, thawed
- 4 dates, pitted
- 1 cup yogurt
- ½ cup water
- 1 teaspoon honey

Preparation method:

1. Slice apricots, bananas and dates.
2. Place into food processor and add blueberries, yogurt and honey.
3. Pulse until roughly combined.
4. Add water and pulse until you have smooth mixture.
5. Serve into tall glasses.

Wheat-free French toast

Serving: 6

Ingredients:

- 1 cup berries, by your choice
- ¼ teaspoon lemon juice
- ¼ teaspoon lemon zest, grated
- 1 egg
- 2 egg whites
- ¼ teaspoon baking powder
- 2 tablespoons sugar
- 4 slices wheat-free bread, cut into 1-inch cubes
- ½ cup milk
- 1 teaspoon vanilla extract
- 1 teaspoon oil

Preparation method:

1. Preheat the oven to 200C/400F and grease 6-inch pan with oil.
2. Combine together berries, sugar, and lemon zest and lemon juice; set aside.
3. Place half of sliced bread cubes into baking pan.
4. Spread over berries and top remaining bread slices.

5. Combine milk, eggs, egg whites, vanilla extract and baking powder.
6. Pour the mixture over prepared dish and bake for 20 minutes or until the liquid has vaporized.
7. Cool before slicing.
8. You can additionally dust with icing sugar.

Buckwheat mini pancakes

Serving: 4

Ingredients:

- ½ cup buckwheat flour
- 1 egg
- 1 cup milk
- ½ cup water
- 1 tablespoon yogurt
- Frying oil

Preparation method:

1. Whisk the egg, flour and milk until you have smooth batter.
2. In another bowl whisk yogurt and water until well combined.
3. Combine these two mixtures and mix until smooth.
4. Heat some oil in non-stick skillet and add 2 tablespoons of batter per pancake.
5. When bubbles appear flip the pancake to other side and cook for 1-2 minutes.
6. Serve with fresh fruits or yogurt.

Simple breakfast plate

Serving: 2

Ingredients:

- 4 oz. cottage cheese
- 5 walnuts, chopped
- 4 dates, chopped
- 1 fig, sliced
- 2 slices wheat free bread
- 1 tablespoon honey

Preparation method:

1. Spread ½ tablespoon of honey per bread slice.
2. Microwave for 30 seconds and set aside.
3. In a small bowl combine cottage cheese, chopped dates and chopped walnuts.
4. Spread the mixture over bread slices and top with sliced fig.
5. Serve immediately.

Healthy breakfast smoothie

Serving: 2

Ingredients:

- ½ cup milk
- ½ banana
- ½ cup frozen raspberries, thawed
- 2 dates

Preparation method:

1. Place all ingredients into food processor.
2. Pulse until well combined.
3. Refrigerate for 20 minutes before serving.
4. Serve in tall glasses and decorate with banana slices.

Potato hash

Serving: 2

Ingredients:

- 2 potatoes, peeled and cut into ½ - inch cubes
- ½ onion diced
- 1 garlic clove, minced
- 1 tablespoon olive oil
- ½ tablespoon butter
- ½ red bell pepper, chopped
- 2 tablespoons grated cheese – by your choice
- Freshly ground salt and pepper

Preparation method:

1. Preheat the butter and oil in medium size non-stick skillet.
2. Add potatoes, bell pepper and toss to coat with oil.
3. Cover the skillet with a lid and cook potatoes for 10 minutes.
4. Remove the lid add onion and season with salt and pepper.
5. Cook for 10 minutes, until all is tender.
6. Add garlic and cook for 2 minutes more.
7. Sprinkle with cheese and let it sit for 2 minutes.
8. Serve immediately.

WHEAT FREE LUNCH RECIPES

Broccoli soup

Serving: 3

Ingredients:

- 1 small bunch broccoli
- 2 tablespoons olive oil
- 2 cups vegetable stock
- Freshly ground salt and pepper
- 1 tablespoon thick yogurt
- 1 small onion, chopped
- ½ teaspoon ground cumin

Preparation method:

1. Heat oil in large skillet and add chopped onion. Cook onion for 10 minutes over medium-high heat or until translucent.
2. Add chopped broccoli and cook for 5 minutes.
3. Add vegetable stock, cumin and cook for 15 minutes or until the broccoli is tender.
4. Transfer all to a food blender or blend with hand blender, until you have smooth and creamy soup.
5. Stir in thick yogurt and serve while still warm.

Canned tuna salad

Serving: 2

Ingredients:

- 1 can tuna, drained
- ½ cup feta cheese, crumbled
- 1 teaspoon dried basil
- 2 bread slices, wheat-free
- 1 garlic clove, minced
- 1 tablespoon olive oil

Preparation method:

1. Combine canned tuna with feta cheese in a bowl.
2. Drizzle with olive oil and sprinkle with basil. Add minced garlic.
3. Toss to combine ad set in refrigerator for 20 minutes.
4. Meanwhile, toast bread slices and cut them into cubes.
5. Add bread cubes to tuna salad and toss gain to combine.
6. Serve immediately.

Wheat-free macaroni and cheese

Serving: 4

Ingredients:

- 12 oz. wheat free pasta (like Heartland corn and rice pasta)
- 2 cups grated cheese – by your choice
- 2 tablespoons butter
- ½ cup cream
- Freshly ground salt
- 2 tablespoons sunflower oil

Preparation method:

1. In a large pot bring 10-12 cups of water to boil. Add salt, sunflower oil and pasta.
2. Cook pasta according to manufactures direction, stirring frequently.
3. When cooked, drain pasta and set aside.
4. In a small sauce pan heat butter over low heat; add grated cheese and cream. Stir until melted.
5. Serve pasta into wide plate and drizzle with cheese sauce.
6. You can additionally sprinkle with cheese.

Simple polenta pizza

Serving: 6

Ingredients:

- 1 pint vegetable stock
- 6 oz. polenta
- 1 tablespoon olive oil
- Freshly ground salt and pepper
- ¼ teaspoon dried basil
- ¼ cup pizza sauce
- 3 Portobello mushrooms, sliced
- 1 tablespoon canned corn

Preparation method:

1. Bring stock to boil in large pot, over high heat.
2. Stir in freshly ground salt and pepper, basil and olive oil.
3. Whisking constantly pour in polenta and continue whisking for 5 minutes, until smooth
4. Pour into greased tart pan and spread evenly. Place in refrigerator for 30 minutes.
5. Meanwhile, preheat the oven to 180C/350F.
6. Remove polenta from the refrigerator, sprinkle baking sheet with cornmeal and transfer polenta pizza crust to the baking sheet.
7. Bake for 40 minutes.

8. Spread over pizza crust pizza sauce, canned corn and mushrooms.
9. Place back in the oven and bake for 15 minutes more.
10. Remove from the oven, cut with pizza wheel and serve.

Corn and black bean salad

Serving: 2

Ingredients:

- ½ cup frozen corn kernels
- 7 oz. can black beans, rinsed
- 2 garlic cloves, minced
- ¼ cup vegetable broth
- 1 tablespoon fresh cilantro, chopped
- ½ brown onion, chopped
- 1 teaspoon vegetable oil

Preparation method:

1. Heat the oil in the non-stick skillet.
2. Add onion and cook until browned.
3. Mix in the garlic and cook for 30 seconds.
4. Add beans, corn and vegetable broth.
5. Cook for 10 minutes or until liquid vaporizes.
6. Remove from the heat and stir in the cilantro.
7. Serve immediately.

Wheat-free ravioli

Serving: 4

Ingredients:

- 1 cup rice flour
- ¼ cup tapioca starch
- 1 egg white
- 3 eggs
- Small pinch of salt

For the filling:

- 1 cup frozen spinach, thawed
- 2 garlic cloves, minced
- ½ cup cottage cheese

Preparation method:

1. Mix rice flour, salt and tapioca starch.
2. Add whisked egg white and eggs, gradually, one by one.
3. Stir until dough starts to separate from the bowl.
4. Divide the dough to 2 equal parts.
5. Roll the dough on floured kitchen surface using rolling pin to ¼ - inch thick or thinner.
6. Using ravioli cutter cut out the raviolis and set them aside.

7. In a small bowl combine thawed spinach, minced garlic and cottage cheese.
8. Spoon the mixture onto prepared raviolis, 1 teaspoon per one ravioli.
9. Brush edges with some water, fold raviolis and press with fingers to seal the edges.
10. Bring a large pot of salted water to boil.
11. Add raviolis in and cook until they float up. This is a sign that they are cooked.
12. Remove raviolis from water and serve into a plate.
13. You can additionally pour over some pasta sauce or white béchamel sauce.

Lentils stew

Serving: 4

Ingredients:

- 6 oz. brown lentil, canned
- ½ small onion, chopped
- Freshly ground salt and pepper
- ½ pound minced beef meat
- 2 oz. canned tomatoes, chopped
- 1 – inch cinnamon stick, crushed
- ½ teaspoon chili flakes
- 1 tablespoon olive oil

Preparation method:

1. Rinse lentils and set aside.
2. Add onion, freshly ground salt and pepper and minced meat into heated pan with olive oil. Cook for 5 minutes.
3. Add lentils, stir to combine and add enough water to cover the lentils and to come over the lentils for around 2 – inches.
4. Heat over medium high heat and bring to simmer.
5. Continue simmering for ½ hour or until the lentils are tender.
6. Add cinnamon stick, chili flakes and simmer additionally for 10 minutes.
7. Serve while still hot in small bowls.

Cheese scones

Serving: 6

Ingredients:

- 7 oz. wheat-free all-purpose flour
- ½ teaspoon wheat-free baking powder
- 2 oz. butter, room temperature
- 1 oz. grated cheese – by your choice
- 1 cup milk
- Small pinch of salt

Preparation method:

1. Preheat the oven to 220C/425F and lightly grease baking pan.
2. Combine together flour, salt and baking powder. Stir in the butter.
3. Add grated cheese and milk. Mix until you have a soft dough.
4. Roll the dough onto lightly floured surface, using rolling pin to ¾ - inch thick.
5. Cut out scones and transfer them onto greased baking tray.
6. Brush scones with some milk and bake for 15 minutes or until golden.
7. Serve when cooled.

Spicy chicken bites

Serving: 2

Ingredients:

- 1 pair chicken breasts
- 1 tablespoon buckwheat flour
- ½ teaspoon smoked paprika
- ½ teaspoon ground cumin
- ½ teaspoon celery salt
- 1 egg, whisked
- Freshly ground salt and pepper
- Vegetable oil, for frying
- 1 cup creamy cheese + 1 tablespoon chives, chopped

Preparation method:

1. Cut the chicken breasts into bite size pieces.
2. Coat chicken bites into buckwheat flour.
3. Combine paprika, cumin, freshly ground pepper and celery salt in shallow dish.
4. Whisk egg in another shallow dish. Dip the floured chicken bites into eggs and into spices.
5. Heat some oil in the non-stick skillet and add chicken bites.
6. Cook the chicken for 3-4 minutes or until golden.
7. Drain chicken well on the clean kitchen towel and serve with mixture of creamy cheese and cilantro.

Wheat-free Yorkshire pudding

Serving: 8

Ingredients:

- ½ cup tapioca flour
- ½ cup rice flour
- 2 eggs
- 2 tablespoons butter, melted
- 1 ¼ cups milk
- Freshly ground salt and pepper
- Some olive oil

Preparation method:

1. Preheat the oven to 230C/45F and line 8-hole muffin tin with olive oil.
2. Sift the tapioca flour and rive flour into the medium size bowl. Add salt and pepper.
3. Make a well in the center and add the eggs.
4. Beat continuously, gradually drawing the flour from the sides, adding half the milk.
5. When beaten, stir in rest of the milk and cooled, melted butter. Set aside for 15 minutes.
6. Meanwhile, heat the muffin tin and when heated scoop the batter into the heated muffin holes, to 2/3 full.
7. Bake for 15 minutes and serve warm.

Wheat-free bacon bean soup

Serving: 3

Ingredients:

- 1 carrot, peeled and grated
- ½ large onion, chopped
- 2 tablespoons olive oil
- 3 thick slices smoked bacon, chopped
- 2 garlic cloves, minced
- 1 bay leaf
- 2 cups canned beans, drained
- ½ quart vegetable stock
- Freshly ground salt and pepper – if needed

Preparation method:

1. Heat olive oil in in medium saucepan. Add carrot and onion and cook until tender.
2. Add the bacon, garlic and bay leaf. Cook for 2-3 minutes.
3. Stir in the beans and cover all with vegetable stock.
4. Bring to boil over medium high heat. Let it boil for 2 minutes, then reduce heat to medium low.
5. Simmer for 20 minutes remove from the heat.

6. When cooled, blend all using hand blender, until you have smooth puree.
7. Serve while still warm and garnish with freshly chopped parsley.

Wheat-free potato scones

Serving: 4

Ingredients:

- 1 large potato – around 7 oz.
- Small pinch of salt
- 1 ½ tablespoons butter, room temperature
- ½ cup rice flour
- 1 teaspoon baking powder
- Some vegetable oil

Preparation method:

1. Peel the potato, cut into chunks and place in pot with boiling water. Cook potatoes until tender than drain, leaving some of the cooking water.
2. Add butter to the potatoes and using potato mash, make fluffy puree.
3. Sift the flour and baking powder into the puree and stir until well combined. Season with salt.
4. Roll the mixture into a ball and place on large piece of parchment paper. Cover with another piece of parchment paper and roll out using roll pin to ¼ - inch thick.

5. Cut into 8 wedges – scones and prick all over with a fork.
6. Heat some oil in large non-stick skillet and transfer the wedges in the skillet as soon as oil is heated.
7. Cook for 5 minutes on each side, or until golden.
8. Serve while still warm.

Wheat-free pumpkin seeds bread

Serving: 8

Ingredients:

- 3 cups porridge oats, processed to a fine flour (use food processor for this)
- 1 teaspoon dry yeast
- 2 teaspoons honey
- Small pinch of salt
- 1 cup warm water
- 1 tablespoon vegetable oil
- 2 tablespoons pumpkin seeds

Preparation method:

1. Preheat the oven to 180C/350F and grease non-stick loaf pan.
2. Combine yeast, honey and salt in small bowl.
3. Combine processed oats, water, oil and mixture of honey and yeast.
4. Knead the dough with floured hands on a floured surface, for 10 minutes.
5. Divide the dough and knead in the pumpkin seeds.
6. Shape the dough and place in the center of loaf pan.

7. Let it raise for 30 minutes in the warm room.
8. Bake in the oven for 50-60 minutes or until firm.
9. Cool before slicing.

Tuna fishcakes wheat-free

Serving: 5

Ingredients:

- 1 cup canned tuna fish, drained
- 3 cups potato puree
- ½ tablespoons butter
- 1 egg, beaten
- ½ cup fine cornmeal
- ½ tablespoon olive oil
- ½ tablespoon chopped parsley
- A dash of Tabasco sauce
- Vegetable oil, for frying
- Freshly ground salt and pepper

Preparation method:

1. Combine tuna, mashed potatoes, Tabasco sauce, parsley, salt and pepper and butter. Mix well until smooth.
2. Dust your hand with corn flour and roll the mixture into patties.
3. Dip each tuna cake into beaten egg, then in cornmeal.
4. Chill in the freezer for 30 minutes.

5. Heat the oil in non-stick skillet and fry tuna cakes for 5 minutes on each side, or until golden.
6. Drain on kitchen towel before serving.

Oven baked potatoes with cottage cheese and garlic

Serving: 4

Ingredients:

- 8 potatoes, small size
- 1 cup cottage cheese
- 1 teaspoon ground cumin
- 1 tablespoon olive oil
- 2 garlic cloves, minced
- 1 cucumber, grated
- Freshly ground salt and pepper

Preparation method:

1. Place potatoes in large pot of water and bring to boil over medium-high heat.
2. Meanwhile, preheat the oven to 200C/420F and grease baking tray with olive oil.
3. Cook potatoes for 15 minutes than drain.
4. Place them in the greased baking tray and press with thumb, so you king of crush them
5. Drizzle with olive oil, season with salt and pepper and ground cumin.

6. Bake in oven for 15 minutes more and set aside.
7. Combine cottage cheese, grated cucumber and minced garlic.
8. Spread over baked potatoes and serve.

Vegetable burgers

Serving: 6

Ingredients:

- ½ cup cooked chickpeas
- ¾ cup frozen veggies, thawed
- 2 tablespoons chickpea flour
- 1 egg white
- 1 garlic clove, minced
- Freshly ground salt and pepper
- Some vegetable oil for frying

Preparation method:

1. Place frozen veggies, chickpea flour, cooked chickpea, egg white and freshly ground salt and pepper into the food processor.
2. Blend until well combined and if needed add more chickpea flour.
3. Grease non-stick skillet with some oil and heat over medium-high heat.
4. Form burgers from prepared mixture and cook for 3 minutes on each side or until golden.
5. Transfer to a plate and serve.

Wheat-free cheese rolls

Serving: 8

Ingredients:

- 1 cup tapioca flour
- ¼ cup rice flour
- 1 ½ teaspoons baking powder
- Small pinch of salt
- 1 teaspoon active dry yeast
- 3 eggs
- 4 tablespoons milk
- 8 oz. shredded cheese – by your choice

Preparation method:

1. Preheat the oven to 190C/375F and grease baking pan with some oil.
2. Place rice flour, tapioca flour, baking powder, yeast, salt and shredded cheese into food processor.
3. Pulse until blended.
4. Add eggs, milk and pulse until you have almost smooth dough.
5. Dust kitchen surface with some tapioca flour and knead dough until smooth.
6. Divide dough into 8 equal parts and form balls.

7. Arrange balls onto prepared baking tray.
8. Cover with plastic foil and let them sit for 30 minutes in a warm room.
9. Bake rolls for 20-25 minutes or until golden.
10. Leave on wire rack to cool and serve while still warm.

Oven roasted veggies

Serving: 4

Ingredients:

- 1 medium zucchini, sliced
- 1 medium eggplant, diced
- 1 teaspoon salt
- 1 can (7 oz.) tomatoes
- 1 small red bell pepper, cut into 1-inch pieces
- 1 medium onion, diced
- 2 garlic cloves, minced
- 1 teaspoon crush coriander seeds
- 2 tablespoons olive oil
- Freshly ground pepper
- 1 teaspoon fresh parsley, chopped

Preparation method:

1. Place zucchini, eggplant and bell pepper in a bowl. Season with salt and drain excess liquid.
2. Arrange drained vegetables and onion on baking tray.
3. Drizzle with olive oil and season with parsley, coriander, black pepper and garlic cloves.
4. Add crushed canned tomatoes and toss all to combine.

5. Preheat the oven to 200C/420F.
6. Bake vegetables for 30-40 minutes or until tender and edges are brown.
7. Serve straight away.

Wheat-free lasagna

Serving: 4

Ingredients:

- 2 sweet potatoes, peeled and sliced to ¼- inch round slices
- 1 onion, sliced into thin round slices
- 2 cups grated cheese – by your choice
- 1 cauliflower, cut into florets
- 3 garlic cloves, minced
- 1 cup tomato sauce
- Freshly ground salt and pepper
- Some olive oil1 teaspoon dried basil

Preparation method:

1. Preheat the oven to 200C/400F.
2. Arrange potato and onion slices onto lined baking sheet with parchment paper, drizzle with olive oil and bake for 10-13 minutes or until tender and brown. Set aside and reduce heat to 180C/350F.
3. Place ¼ cup of tomato sauce in the bottom of lasagna baking dish.
4. Layer the potatoes and onion. Cover with ¼ cup tomato sauce and 1/3 grated cheese.
5. Add another layer of tomatoes, onion and repeat the previous steps.

6. Top with cauliflower, minced garlic, remaining sauce and remaining cheese.
7. Bake at 180C/350F for 30-35 minutes.
8. Let it cool before serving.

WHEAT FREE DINNER RECIPES

Cheese casserole

Serving: 4

Ingredients:

- 2 bell peppers, thinly sliced
- 1 cup chopped onion
- 1 garlic clove, minced
- 2 tablespoons olive oil
- 10 oz. can diced tomatoes
- 3 eggs
- 5 3gg whites
- ¼ cup wheat-free all-purpose flour
- ½ teaspoon baking powder
- ¼ cup crumbled feta cheese
- ¼ cup grated cheese, like cheddar
- Freshly ground salt

Preparation method:

1. Heat olive oil in large non-stick skillet. Add onion and cook until glassy.
2. Add garlic and cook for 1 minute.
3. Add the tomatoes and bring to simmer; gently simmer for 15 minutes.
4. Preheat the oven to 180C/350F and pour the prepared tomato sauce in the bottom of baking dish.

5. Layer the bell peppers onto tomato sauce. Top with feta cheese,
6. In a large bowl combine eggs, egg whites, flour, baking powder and salt.
7. Pour the mixture over the bell peppers and sprinkle with cheddar cheese.
8. Bake for 30 minutes, covered and for 10 minutes uncovered. It should be golden with brown edges.
9. Serve with some thick yogurt.

Garlic hummus

Serving: 3

Ingredients:

- 2 cups cooked chickpeas
- 2 tablespoons sesame paste
- Juice of 1 lemon
- 2 tablespoons olive oil
- Small pinch of salt
- 2 garlic bulbs, medium size
- ¼ cup water

Preparation method:

1. Preheat the oven to 180C/350F.
2. Cut off the top of garlic bulbs, and coat with some olive oil.
3. Wrap bulbs in aluminum foil and bake for 50 minutes. Set aside.
4. When cooled squeeze the soft garlic from cloves.
5. Place in the food processor and add chickpea.
6. Add rest of ingredients; sesame paste, lemon juice, olive oil, salt and water.
7. Pulse until well combined.
8. If needed add more olive oil, until you have creamy paste.
9. Sprinkle with some smoked paprika before serving.

Green beans with garlic

Serving: 2

Ingredients:

- 10 oz. green beans, trimmed
- 3 garlic cloves, sliced
- 2 tablespoons olive oil
- Freshly ground salt and pepper
- ¼ cup thick yogurt

Preparation method:

1. Cook the green beans in pot of boiling water, for 3 minutes or until tender.
2. Drain well and set aside.
3. Heat olive oil in large skillet and add sliced garlic.
4. Cook for 1 minute and add green beans. Season with salt and pepper. Toss to combine.
5. Serve immediately with fresh yogurt.

Brussels sprouts and chestnuts

Serving: 2

Ingredients:

- 13 oz. Brussels sprouts
- 1 cup roasted chestnuts
- 1 tablespoon apple cider vinegar
- 1 tablespoon olive oil
- Small pinch of sea salt
- Freshly ground pepper
- 1 teaspoon smoked paprika

Preparation method:

1. Preheat the oven to 200C/400F and grease baking pan with olive oil.
2. Add Brussels sprouts, olive oil, smoked paprika, sea salt, pepper and apple vinegar. Toss to combine.
3. Bake for 20 minutes and remove from the oven.
4. Add chestnuts and again toss to combine. Bake for additional 10 minutes and serve.

Chestnut carrot soup

Serving: 4

Ingredients:

- 1 cup cooked chestnuts
- 1 cup chopped carrots
- 1 tablespoon butter
- 1 tablespoon olive oil
- 1 chopped onion
- 4 cups vegetable stock
- Freshly ground salt and pepper
- 1 celery stalk, sliced

Preparation method:

1. Melt butter in a sauce pan with olive oil over medium high heat.
2. Add carrots, onion, sliced celery and cook for 5 minutes.
3. Add chestnuts, salt and pepper and vegetable stock.
4. Cover and simmer for 20 minutes.
5. Using hand blender, blend all ingredients until smooth.
6. Bring it to boil, for 1 minute and remove from the heat.
7. Serve in a small bowls and garnish with some parsley.

Brown rice and tuna salad

Serving: 4

Ingredients:

- 1 cup cooked brown rice
- 2 tablespoons olive oil
- Juice from ½ lemon
- 1 tablespoon sherry vinegar
- 6 oz. canned tuna
- 1 spring onion
- 1 cup cooked snow peas, cut to bite pieces
- 2 springs mint, chopped
- 2 hardboiled eggs, cut into wedges
- Freshly ground salt and pepper.

Preparation method:

1. Whisk the olive oil, vinegar and lemon juice. Add freshly ground salt and pepper. Set aside.
2. Combine tuna and cooked rice. Serve onto plate.
3. In another bowl combine finely sliced spring onion, mint and snow peas.
4. Spread the bean mixture over the rice, top with egg wedges and drizzle over olive oil-lemon juice dressing.
5. Serve immediately.

Zucchini pie

Serving: 4

Ingredients:

- ¼ cup wheat-free bread crumbs
- 2 garlic cloves, minced
- 1 onion, chopped
- 2 tablespoon butter
- 1 tablespoon olive oil
- 2 small tomatoes, seeded and diced
- 3 zucchinis, quartered lengthwise and thinly sliced
- 3 eggs
- ½ cup milk
- Freshly ground salt and pepper
- 3 tablespoons Parmesan cheese
- ¼ lb. cheddar cheese

Preparation method:

1. Preheat the oven to 180C/375F and grease baking disk with ½ tablespoon butter.
2. Sprinkle bottom and sides of baking dish with bread crumbs and set aside.
3. Heat rest of butter with olive oil and sauté garlic and onion, until glassy.
4. Stir in diced tomatoes and cook for 5 minutes.

5. Add zucchinis and season with salt and pepper. Cook zucchinis for 5 minutes.
6. Remove from the heat and set aside.
7. Whisk the eggs with the milk. Add zucchini mixture and stir until combined.
8. Pour half of the mixture into prepared baking tray. Top with cheddar cheese and add rest of zucchini mixture.
9. Top with parmesan cheese.
10. Bake for 30-35 minutes.
11. Let it rest before slicing.
12. Serve while still warm.

Broccoli quiche

Serving: 4

Ingredients:

- 1 cup broccoli
- 1 cup cheddar cheese
- ¼ cup onion, diced
- 1 ½ cups milk
- 3 eggs
- ½ cup potato flour
- 1 teaspoon baking powder
- Freshly ground salt and pepper

Preparation method:

1. Place broccoli, onion and cheese in food processor.
2. Pulse until well combined.
3. Preheat the oven to 180C/350F and grease baking dish with some cooking oil.
4. Transfer broccoli mixture to prepared baking dish.
5. Whisk eggs, milk, flour, baking powder and freshly ground salt and pepper.
6. Pour over broccoli mixture and place in the oven.
7. Bake for 45 minutes.
8. Let it slightly cool before slicing and serving.

Asparagus and tomato risotto

Serving: 2

Ingredients:

- 2 tablespoons olive oil
- 2 garlic cloves, minced
- 1 cup
- ¼ lb. fresh asparagus, trimmed and blanched
- ½ cup tomatoes, diced
- 4 cups chicken broth
- 1 teaspoon basil
- 2 tablespoons butter
- ¼ cup shredded Cheddar cheese
- 1 tablespoon chopped parsley

Preparation method:

1. Heat the oil in large non-stick pan over medium heat.
2. Add garlic and cook for 2-3 minutes.
3. Stir in rice and cook for 2-3 minutes.
4. Add ½ cup broth and stir until completely absorbed.
5. Repeat the process of adding the broth until all the broth is absorbed.
6. Add asparagus to the risotto. Stir well.

7. Stir in the cheese, butter and basil.
8. Right before serving add diced tomatoes.
9. Transfer to a large bowl and garnish with parsley.

WHEAT FREE DESSERT RECIPES

Wheat-free pumpkin pie

Serving: 8

Ingredients:

- ¾ cup rice flour
- ½ cup all-purpose wheat-free flour
- ½ cup butter, room temperature
- 2 egg yolks
- 1 tablespoon water
- 2 tablespoons sugar
- 1 cup pumpkin puree
- 2 tablespoons sugar
- 1 egg, beaten
- ¾ cup evaporated milk
- ¼ teaspoon nutmeg
- ½ teaspoon cinnamon

Preparation method:

1. Preheat the oven to 220C/425F and grease tart tin with some butter and dust with rice flour.
2. In a large bowl combine rice flour, wheat-free flour and sugar. Stir well.
3. Add softened butter and knead with hands until you have crumbly mixture.

4. Add egg yolks, water and knead with hands until you have smooth dough.
5. On a lightly floured surface roll out the dough, to ¼-inch thick.
6. Transfer the rolled dough to tart tin and slightly press the dough into tart tin. Trim off the edges and set in refrigerator for 30 minutes.
7. Preparing the filling; combine pumpkin puree, cinnamon, nutmeg and sugar in a small bowl.
8. Add beaten egg and evaporated milk. Stir well to combine until you have smooth mixture.
9. Pour the mixture into prepared dough shell and bake for 15 minutes. Reduce heat to 180C/350F and bake for 30-35 minutes, or until the pie filling is set.
10. When baked, allow cooling at the room temperature.
11. Cut into 8 slices and serve.

Peanut butter and oatmeal slices

Serving: 12 pieces

Ingredients:

- 1 cup cooking oat
- 2 tablespoons sugar
- ½ teaspoon baking soda
- Small pinch of salt
- 1 teaspoon vanilla extract
- ¼ cup milk
- 1 egg, beaten
- 1 small banana, mashed
- ¼ cup peanut butter

Preparation method:

1. Preheat the oven to 180C/350F and line baking tray with parchment paper.
2. Combine cooking oat, sugar salt and baking powder.
3. Add peanut butter and banana. Stir well until combined.
4. Spread the mixture onto prepared baking sheet and flatten with spatula.
5. Bake for 20-22 minutes or until golden.
6. Cut into squares and keep in airtight container.

Buckwheat raisin and cinnamon rolls

Serving: 8 rolls

Ingredients:

- 1 ½ cups buckwheat flour
- 2 tablespoons butter
- ½ cup thick yogurt
- 2 tablespoons milk
- 1 egg + 1 egg white
- 1 tablespoon honey
- ¼ cup sugar
- 1 tablespoon butter
- 1 tablespoon cinnamon
- 2 tablespoons raisins
- ¼ teaspoon cardamom

Preparation method:

1. Preheat the oven to 180/350F and line baking tray with parchment paper.
2. Place the butter and buckwheat flour in food processor. Blend until you have crumbly dough.
3. Add yogurt, honey and eggs.
4. Pulse until you have smooth batter.

5. Knead the dough on lightly floured surface and wrap in plastic foil. Set in refrigerator for 30 minutes.
6. Meanwhile, prepare the filling; Combine the butter, cinnamon and cardamom.
7. Roll the chilled dough between two parchment papers, using rolling pin to ¼-inch thick and rectangular shape.
8. Spread the cinnamon filling over the dough and sprinkle with raisins.
9. Firmly roll the dough into log shape and cut into 8 portions. Brush with milk.
10. Arrange rolls onto baking sheet and bake for 20-25 minutes or until golden.
11. Serve when cooled.

Coconut balls

Serving: 12

Ingredients:

- 1 cup shredded coconut, unsweetened
- 3 tablespoons coconut oil
- 3 tablespoons caster sugar
- 1 teaspoon vanilla extract
- Small pinch of salt

Preparation method:

1. Place shredded coconut, coconut oil, sugar and vanilla extract in a food processor.
2. Ass salt and pulse until mixture is blended and it stick together.
3. Remove the mixture from the blender and form walnut size balls.
4. Arrange onto baking tray lined with parchment paper and set in refrigerator for 1 hour.
5. Before serving you can drizzle with some melted chocolate.

Simple chocolate yogurt

Serving: 2

Ingredients:

- 1 cup plain thick yogurt
- 2 teaspoons unsweetened liquid cocoa
- ¼ teaspoon cardamom
- 1 tablespoon honey

Preparation method:

1. Combine honey, cardamom and liquid cocoa.
2. Add thick yogurt and stir until well blended.
3. Refrigerate for 20 minutes and serve.
4. You can additionally sprinkle with some cocoa powder.

Wheat-free muffins

Serving: 12

Ingredients:

- 1 cup cooked oatmeal
- 1 egg
- 1 tablespoon butter, melted
- ½ cup milk
- 4 tablespoons honey
- 1 teaspoon baking powder
- Small pinch of salt
- 1 cup wheat-free all-purpose flour
- ¼ cup raisins

Preparation method:

1. Preheat the oven to 18'C/350F and line 12-hole muffin tin with paper cases.
2. Place all ingredients in food processor.
3. Pulse until mixture is well blended and without visible traces of flour.
4. Spoon the mixture into prepared paper cases to 2/3 full.
5. Bake for 25-30 minutes or until brown and firm to the touch.
6. Cool before removing from the muffin tin.

Wheat-free brownies

Serving: 8 pieces

Ingredients:

- 9 oz. black beans, rinsed and drained
- ¼ cup sugar
- 1 egg
- 2 tablespoons butter, melted
- 2 tablespoons cocoa powder
- 1 teaspoon vanilla extract
- Small pinch of salt
- ¼ cup chocolate chips
- 2 tablespoons chopped walnuts

Preparation method:

1. Preheat the oven to 180C/350F and spray the 8x8 non-stick pan.
2. Place the beans, egg, sugar, melted butter, cocoa, salt and vanilla in food processor.
3. Pulse until well combined and scrape the batter from the sides of the bowl.
4. Stir in the chocolate chips and walnuts.
5. Transfer the batter into greased pan and spread evenly.
6. Bake for 25-30 minutes or until slightly puffed.
7. Cool before slicing.

Oat banana cookies

Serving: 12 pieces

Ingredients:

- 1 ½ ripe bananas
- ¼ cup peanut butter
- 2 tablespoon canola oil
- ½ teaspoon vanilla extract
- 1 cup quick oats
- ½ teaspoon baking powder
- ¼ cup chocolate chips
- ¼ teaspoon cinnamon

Preparation method:

1. Preheat the oven to 180C/350F and line baking tray with parchment paper.
2. In the large bowl mash the bananas with peanut butter, vanilla extract and oil.
3. In another bowl combine oats, baking powder, cinnamon and salt.
4. Combine wet and dry mixture and add chocolate chips. Stir well.
5. Drop spoonful of mixture onto lined baking sheet, ½-inch apart.
6. Bake for 12-14 minutes and serve when cooled.
7. Keep in airtight container.

Wheat-free cheese cake

Serving: 8

Ingredients:

- 3 cups crushed wheat-free cakes
- ¼ cup butter, room temperature
- 1 tablespoon milk
- 3 cups cream cheese
- 2 tablespoons cornstarch
- 1 egg
- ¼ cup caster sugar
- 1/3 cup sweet whipping cream
- 1 teaspoon vanilla extract

Preparation method:

1. Preheat the oven to 180C/350F and line 9-inch spring release cake tin with parchment paper.
2. Place the crushed biscuits into food processor. Add the melted butter, milk and pulse until well combined.
3. Transfer to the cake tin and use the back of metal spoon to compress.
4. Bake the base for 10 minutes and remove from the oven.

5. Prepare the filling; Combine cheese, cornstarch and sugar in a bowl. Beat until well combined.
6. Add the egg and beat using hand mixer, until well incorporated.
7. Add the vanilla extract and continue beating for 2 minutes until fluffy.
8. Pour the filling over baked cake crust and smooth the top with silicone spatula.
9. Bake the cake for 35-40 minutes and make sure it does not turn too brown. It should be golden and pale brown.
10. Remove from the oven and let it cool for 1 hour before slicing.
11. You can drizzle the cake with caramel topping before serving.

Apple dessert

Serving: 4

Ingredients:

- 1 cup walnuts
- ½ tablespoon butter
- ¼ teaspoon salt

For the filling:

- 4 cup chopped apples
- 1 tablespoon butter
- 2 tablespoons honey
- 2 tablespoons rice flour
- ½ teaspoon cinnamon
- ½ teaspoon cardamom

Preparation method:

1. Preheat the oven to 180C/350F and line baking tray with parchment paper.
2. Combine walnuts with butter and salt. Pour onto lined baking sheet and bake for 15 minutes.
3. Place them in food processor and process until coarse, crumbly meal forms. Set aside.
4. Preparing the filling; melt the butter in small sauce pan.

5. Add apples, spices and honey.
6. Simmer for 20 minutes over medium-low heat or until the apples are tender.
7. Stir in the rice flour and cook for 2 minutes and remove from the heat.
8. Place couple spoonful of the walnut crust into glass or small bowl.
9. Top with apples and garnish with cinnamon.

WHEAT FREE SNACK RECIPES

Roasted chickpeas

Serving: 2

Ingredients:

- 1 cup chickpeas, canned
- 1 tablespoon olive oil
- 2 teaspoons curry powder
- Freshly ground salt

Preparation method:

1. Preheat the oven to 200C/400F and line baking tray with parchment paper.
2. Drain, rinse and dry chickpea in kitchen towel.
3. Place chickpea in a medium bowl. Drizzle with olive oil and season with curry powder and salt.
4. Toss to combine and coat chickpeas.
5. Spread onto baking sheet and roast for 30 minutes.
6. Cool before serving.

Baked sweet potatoes

Serving: 2

Ingredients:

- 2 sweet potatoes
- 2 tablespoons olive oil
- 1 teaspoon ground cumin
- Freshly ground salt and pepper

Preparation method:

1. Preheat the oven to 220C/450F and line baking tray with parchment paper.
2. Wash sweet potatoes and peel them.
3. Halve the sweet potatoes lengthwise and cut each again into half, so you have potato fries.
4. Place them onto baking sheet and drizzle with olive oil.
5. Sprinkle with cumin and season with freshly ground salt and pepper.
6. Bake for 15 minutes and then flip to other side, using spatula.
7. Bake for additional 5-10 minutes, depending on their thickness.
8. Sprinkle again with some salt and serve when cooled slightly.

Apple chips

Serving: 2

Ingredients:

- 2 apples, medium size
- 1 teaspoon sugar
- 1 teaspoon cinnamon
- ½ lemon zest, grated

Preparation method:

1. Preheat the oven to 190C/200F and line baking tray with parchment paper.
2. Wash apples well, but do not peel them.
3. Cut apples to 1/8 – inch thick round slices.
4. In a shallow dish combine sugar, cinnamon and lemon zest.
5. Add apples and toss to combine.
6. Arrange apple slices onto baking sheet and bake for 1 hour or until crispy.
7. Remove from the oven and let apple slices cool.
8. Keep in zip lock bag.

Fruit kebabs

Serving: 6

Ingredients:

- 2 ripe bananas
- 5 strawberries
- 2 apricots
- ¼ cup white chocolate chips, melted over steam
- 2 tablespoon coconut flakes
- 6 toothpicks or smaller skewers

Preparation method:

1. Slice bananas, halve strawberries and dice the apricots.
2. Assemble fruit onto skewers: first banana slice, then halved strawberry and finally apricot.
3. Drizzle with melted white chocolate and sprinkle immediately with coconut flakes.
4. Serve as soon as possible.

Yogurt bites

Serving: 4

Ingredients:

- 1 cup thick yogurt
- ¼ cup frozen raspberries, thawed
- 1 tablespoon honey

Preparation method:

1. Blend thick yogurt with honey and thawed raspberries in a food processor.
2. Spoon the mixture into piping bag, with smaller round nozzle.
3. Pipe out the mixture onto lined baking tray with parchment paper and set in freezer for 1 hour or until firm.
4. Serve and consume immediately.

Conclusion

I hope sincerely you enjoyed this book!

It is my deep desire that you enjoy a life full of energy and vitality!

Keep creating new recipes and having fun with the process!

Go wheat free!

Did you like this book?

If you enjoyed this book - please give your review on Amazon about it!

When you turn the page, Kindle will give you the opportunity to rate the book and share your thoughts on Facebook and Twitter. If you believe this book is worth sharing, would you take a few seconds to let your friends know about it? If it turns out to make a difference in their lives, they'll be forever grateful to you.

As I will.

All the best,

Morgan White

Other Books by Morgan White

7027766R00060

Printed in Great Britain
by Amazon.co.uk, Ltd.,
Marston Gate.